TAP DANCING ON THE ROOF

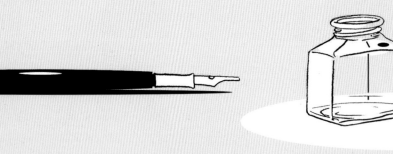

In memory of Joe Dobbin, the inimitable Mórdad
—L.S.P.

To all the kids around the world who cannot read!
— I.B.

Text copyright © 2007 by Linda Sue Park
Illustrations copyright © 2007 by Istvan Banyai

www.hmhco.com

The text of this book is set in 12.5-point ITC Century Schoolbook Condensed.
The illustrations are digital.

The Library of Congress has cataloged the hardcover edition as follows:
Park, Linda Sue.
Tap dancing on the roof : sijo (poems) / by Linda Sue Park ; illustrated by Istvan Banyai.
p. cm.
1. Sijo—United States. 2. Children's poetry, American. I. Banyai, Istvan, ill. II. Title.
PS3566.A6739 T37 2007
811'.54—dc22 2006024901

ISBN: 978-0-618-23483-7 hardcover
ISBN: 978-0-544-55551-8 paperback

Manufactured in Malaysia
TWP 10 9 8 7 6 5 4 3
4500723330

TAP DANCING ON THE ROOF

SIJO* (POEMS) BY
LINDA SUE PARK

*SIJO = a Korean form of poetry

PICTURES BY
ISTVAN BANYAI

HOUGHTON MIFFLIN HARCOURT
BOSTON   NEW YORK

ABOUT SIJO

All the poems in this book are *sijo*. Sijo is a traditional Korean form of poetry. Like a Japanese *haiku,* a *sijo* is written using a syllabic structure. In its most common form, a sijo in English has three lines, each with fourteen to sixteen syllables. (For a fuller explanation, please see the Author's Note.)

Because the lines can be quite long on the page, sijo in English are sometimes divided into six shorter lines. (Some translators believe that a five-line structure more closely matches the old Korean songs from which sijo evolved.) The sijo in this collection are presented in both the three-line and six-line formats.

Each line in a sijo has a special purpose. The first line introduces the topic. The second line develops the topic further. And the third line always contains some kind of twist—humor or irony, an unexpected image, a pun, or a play on words.

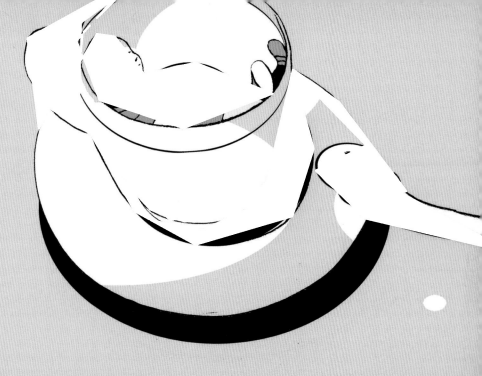

Breakfast

For this meal, people like what they like, the same every morning.
Toast and coffee. Bagel and juice. Cornflakes and milk in a white bowl.

Or—warm, soft, and delicious—a few extra minutes in bed.

LONG DIVISION

This number gets a wall and a ceiling. Nice and comfy in there. But a bunch of other numbers are about to disrupt the peace— bumping the wall, digging up the cellar, tap dancing on the roof.

$$\frac{V^2}{C^2}$$

126,782.54

SCHOOL LUNCH

Each food plopped by tongs or spatula
into its own little space—
square pizza here, square brownie there;
milk carton cube, rectangle tray.

My snack at home after school?
Anything without corners.

ART CLASS

Keesha says my fish doesn't look like anything she's ever seen.
"Flowered fins? *Plaid* scales? And the tail—tie-dyed weirdo green?"

In this ocean, I am Queen. That tail, my dear, is aquamarine.

october

The wind rearranges the leaves,
as if to say, "Much better *there,*"
and coaxes others off their trees:
"It's lots more fun in the air."

Then it plays tag with a plastic bag,
and with one gust uncombs my hair!

POCKETS

What's in your pockets right now? I hope they're not empty:
Empty pockets, unread books, lunches left on the bus—all a waste.
In mine: One horse chestnut. One gum wrapper. One dime. One hamster.

ECHO

Haven't heard that song since preschool,
but I can still sing every word.

Another tune trapped in my head:
Again . . . and again . . . and again . . .

Always playing tricks on me,
those great friends, music and memory.

November Thursday

I don't often talk to my stomach,
but this morning I do:
"Rest up, now. Relax, get ready,
because you will need to S – T – R – E – T – C – H . . ."

Turkey! Pie! And—best of all—
stuffing myself with stuffing!

WORD WATCH

Jittery seems a nervous word;
snuggle curls up around itself.
Some words fit their meanings so well:
Abrupt. Airy. And my favorite—

sesquipedalian,
which means: having lots of syllables.

overnight

Flying saucer poised for liftoff where the bird bath used to be.
On the driveway, three hippos—a mother and two babies.

Snow waves its magic wand: Yesterday, mailbox. Today, hunchback gnome.

VANISHING ACT

Last week I built a snow family. Today, a stubborn sun shines.
My snow people look tired, then sad. . . . I hate seeing them this way.

If that sun shines again tomorrow, I'll find three carrots on the ground.

From the Window

Sparrows at the feeder each day, dull in brown and black and gray
but fun to watch as they scold and eat. One morning, a triple treat—
a primary-colored display: cardinal, goldfinch, blue jay!

crocuses

They pierce the thin skin of snow
with narrow swords of green
to clear the way for colors—
purple, yellow, lavender,

petals huddled close, guarding
the treasure: a lode of gold dust.

IMPORTANT ANNOUNCEMENT

Daffodils blare out the news.
Birds chatter, squirrels jabber,
all ecstatic—*Spring is here!*
Except for the apple tree,
who wakes late, stretches, shakes herself,
makes one last drift of pale-pink snow.

FROG

How proud you are of your strong legs!
Bend and straighten, kick and swim;
soon you will use them to climb
from cool water to sun-warm rock.

But do you wonder where it's gone—
the tail that once served you so well?

summer storm

Lightning jerks the sky awake to take her photograph, *flash!*
Which draws grumbling complaints or even crashing tantrums from thunder—

He hates having his picture taken, so he always gets there late.

ocean EMOTION

The red flag waves its stern warning:
DANGER—NO SWIMMING TODAY.
The ocean churns, foams, roars, dashes,
hurls huge breakers at the sand!

The next day it's all tired out
and takes a long nap in the sun.

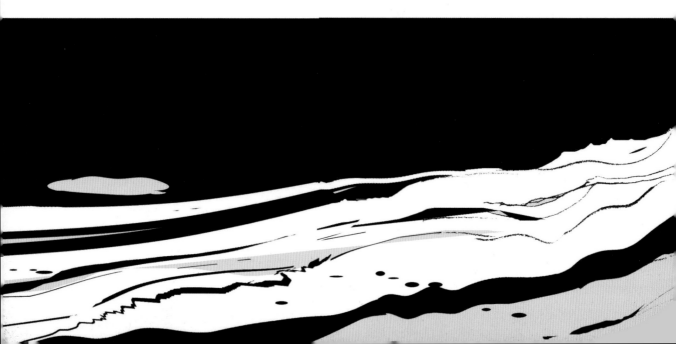

souvenirs

In the shop there are baskets of sand dollars, white and round and smooth.
On the beach I search hard but find only shards, never a whole one.

Are all the perfect sand dollars locked away somewhere—in sand banks?

TIDE LINE

While I sleep, Moon hauls the heavy waves to just the right spot.

On my morning walk, I see how she's redecorated the beach:
The sand freshly scalloped. New fringes of kelp. Shells rearranged.

tennis

When the professionals play,
it's like watching a metronome:
Racquet to racquet and back again,
the ball keeps a perfect, steady beat.

When I'm on the court with my friends,
we improvise: jazz, hip-hop.

1–0

DEFENDER

Everyone wants to get the ball,
run with it, and score a goal.
But when we win one–nothing,
that "nothing" means everything.

It's tough, playing for nothing.
Defense: Intense immense suspense.

BOTANY LESSON

Mom pampers her houseplants, talks to them,
tells them to stand up tall.
But sometimes they give up, lie down, go brown.
They should learn from the weeds—
pushing through the pavement cracks,
smart, tough. Keeping at it, staying green.

LAUNDRY

I love sitting among the heaps of warm, soft, clean-smelling clothes.
My mom folds. I try to match socks, imagining them in Heaven:

Cries of surprise, then celebration! Joyful reunions!

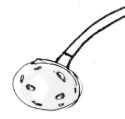

shower

Hurry, wash fast, sister's used up most of the hot water again.
Soap, scrub, rinse. Rub and wrap. Hair shining, skin glowing, smelling fine:
From a tiled cocoon, a butterfly with terrycloth wings.

BEDTIME SNACKS

Good: Cookies and one glass of milk
for two dunkers—me and my dad.

Better: Popcorn, a video,
and sleeping bags stuffed with friends.

Best: Blanket pulled up over my head—
book, flashlight, and chocolate bar.

BRUSHING

Whenever I forget, my dad makes me get out of my warm bed.
The bathroom light is too bright. I squint, squeeze out too much toothpaste.
I wish I could skip it, just once. . . . Eshkoozh me, I can't shpeak jush now.

DAY'S END

All around, the volume turns down low.
The dark grows gently to fill
each room with peace, and me with sleep.
My mind slips out to play . . .

. . . in a world without walls.
Kaleidoscope . . . Calliope . . . Collage!

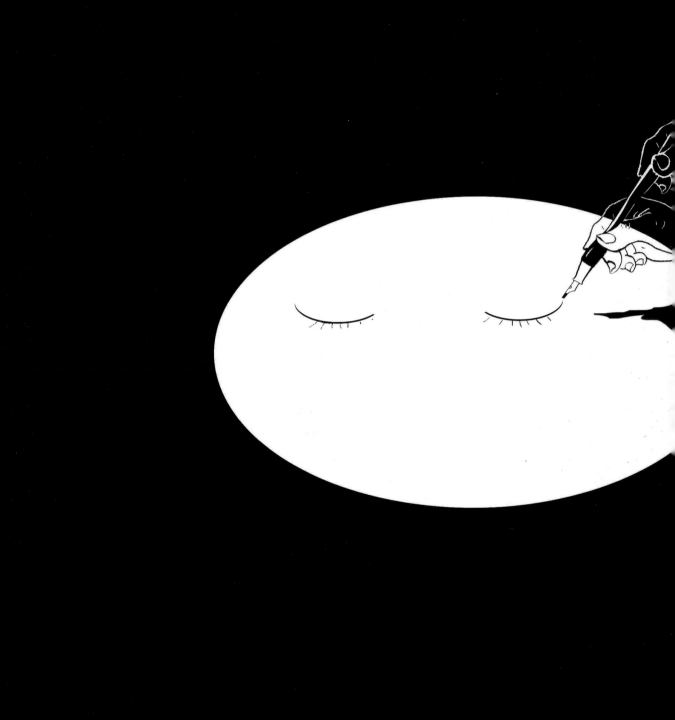

Author's Note

While many poets and readers expect "syllabic" verse forms like haiku and sijo in English to contain a specified number of syllables, the Asian tradition places more importance on the number of stresses. A haiku in Japanese has two stressed syllables in the first line, three in the second, and two in the third. Similarly, each line of a sijo in Korean has two halves, with three stresses in one half and four in the other.

Historical Background

Sijo-like poems were written as early as the sixth century B.C. Originally, they were songs with musical accompaniment, and some are still performed this way today. The songs often praised the beauty of the seasons.

Following the invention of the Korean alphabet (*hangul*) in 1446, the lyrics of such songs were written down, and sijo was eventually accepted as a poetic form. Because hangul is very easy to learn to read and write, these short poems soon became accessible and popular among both poets and readers.

The subject matter of sijo also expanded to encompass a wide range of topics. Unlike traditional haiku, which are limited to topics about nature, sijo are written about personal experience, relationships, and everyday moments, as well as depicting the natural world.

Here is an example of a traditional sijo:

> I like you, bamboo, for you are the truest of true friends.
> When I was young, I made you into stilts and played on you.
> Now you wait outside my window, until I need a walking stick.

—Kim Kwang-uk (1580–1656)

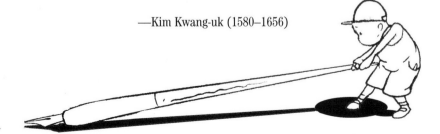

In the sixteenth and seventeenth centuries, women who worked as singers and entertainers for the king and his court developed a tradition of sijo written about love and romance. The body of work created by these courtesans—many of them anonymous —makes sijo one of the few poetic forms with a strong legacy of women poets.

Koreans are proud of sijo's long history and popular appeal. It is a form that I think deserves to be more widely used and better known.

For Further reading

The only collection of sijo for young readers in English that I know of is Virginia Olson Baron's *Sunset in a Spider Web* (New York: Henry Holt & Co., 1974; out of print).

Other collections:

Contogenis, Constantine, and Wolhee Choe. *Songs of the Kisaeng.* Rochester, N.Y.: BOA Editions, 1997.

Kim, Jaihiun, trans. *Classical Korean Poetry.* Fremont, Calif.; Asian Humanities Press, 1994.

Ko, Won, ed. *Contemporary Korean Poetry.* Iowa City: Univ. of Iowa Press, 1970.

Lee, Peter H., ed. and trans. *Anthology of Korean Poetry.* New York: John Day Co., 1964.

Rutt, Richard, ed. and trans. *The Bamboo Grove.* Ann Arbor: Univ. of Michigan Press, 1998.

Finally, a fascinating and extensive explanation of the justification for the five-line structure for sijo in English is presented in one of the more recent collections of sijo available in the U.S.: O'Rourke, Kevin, ed. and trans. *The Book of Korean Shijo.* Cambridge and London: Harvard University Asia Center, 2002.

SOME TIPS FOR WRITING YOUR OWN SIJO

🖋 If you choose to write in the three-line format, each line should contain about fourteen to sixteen syllables. Some writers might find it easier to use the six-line format, where each line should contain seven or eight syllables.

🖋 Advanced poets can try working with the stress count instead of with syllables. In this case, each line should have two halves, with three stresses in one half and four in the other (either 3 / 4 or 4 / 3). An even more sophisticated structure is the five-line format, in which the fourth line is always exactly three syllables. This structure attempts to echo in English the rhythm of traditional sijo, which were sung. (For further explication, please see O'Rourke, as cited in For Further Reading.)

🖋 Start with a single image or idea. Try to make the first line a complete unit of thought. This is easiest to do by writing it as one sentence.

🖋 In the second line, develop the image further by adding details, description, or examples. Again, think of this line as a single unit or sentence.

🖋 Most poets regard the last line—the "twist"—as the hardest part of writing sijo. I try to think of where the poem would go logically if I continued to develop the idea of the first two lines. Once I've figured that out, I write something that goes in the opposite direction—or at least "turns a corner." For example, in "Breakfast," the logical extension would be another line about eating. Instead, the poem ends with an image of sleeping.

🖋 Sijo are traditionally not titled, but modern poets often title their poems, as I do mine.

🖋 Sijo can rhyme or not, as the writer chooses. "Art Class" is an example of sijo using end rhymes. "October" and "From the Window" contain both internal and end rhymes.

I hope the sijo in this collection will inspire readers to try writing their own.

WISH

For someone to read a poem
again, and again, and then,

having lifted it from page
to brain—the easy part—

cradle it on the longer trek
from brain all the way to heart.

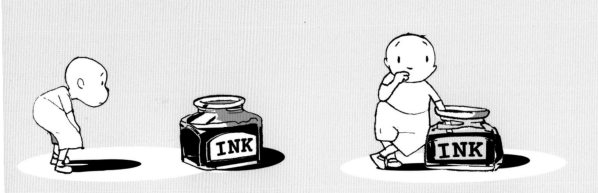